3

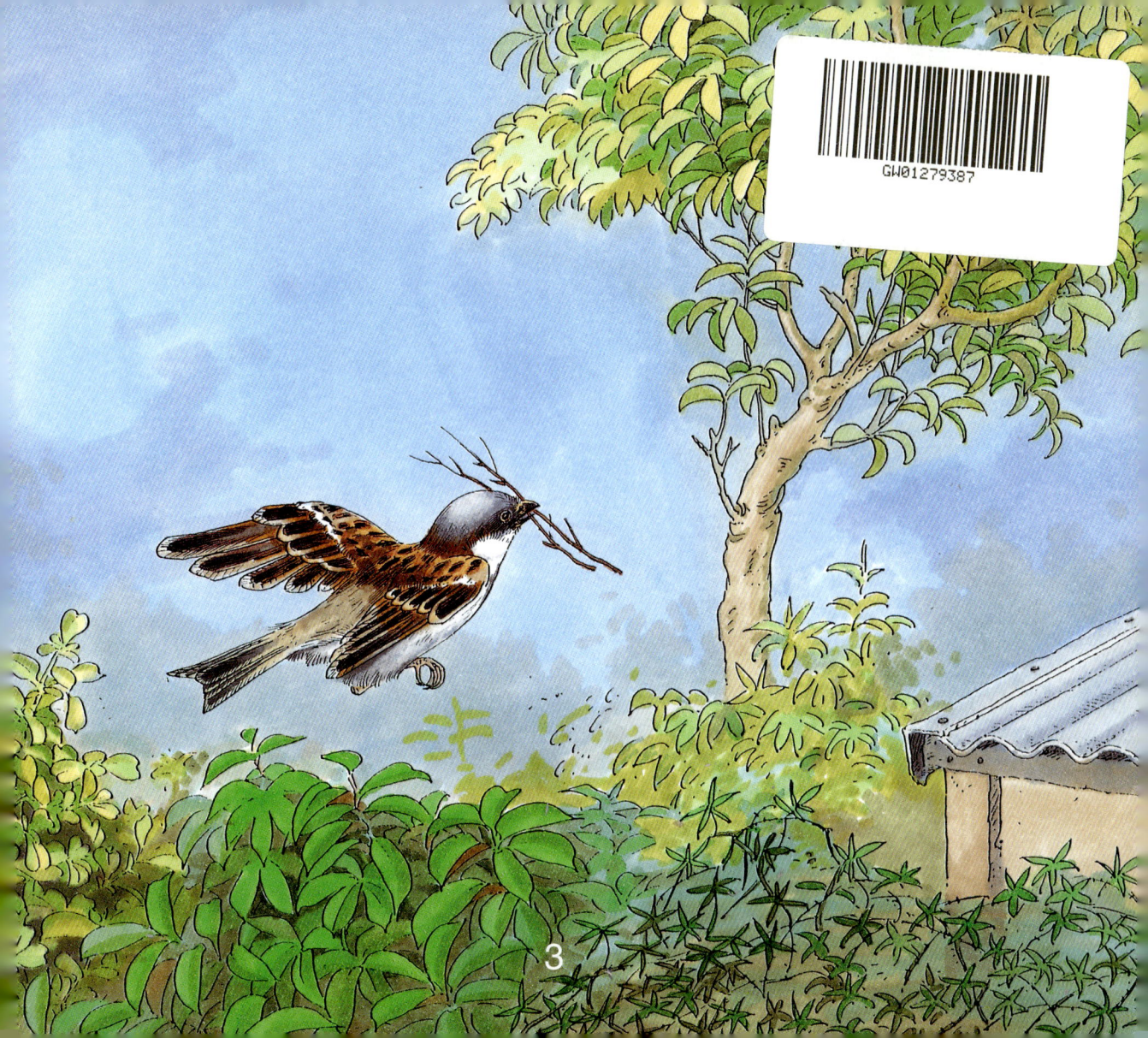

Look! Some grass.

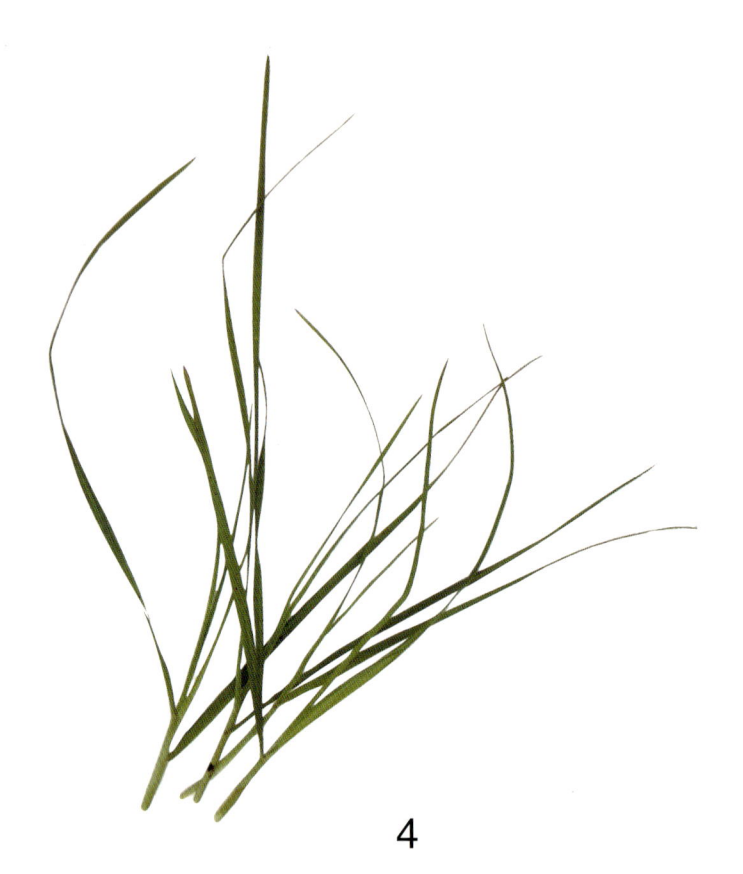

The Nest

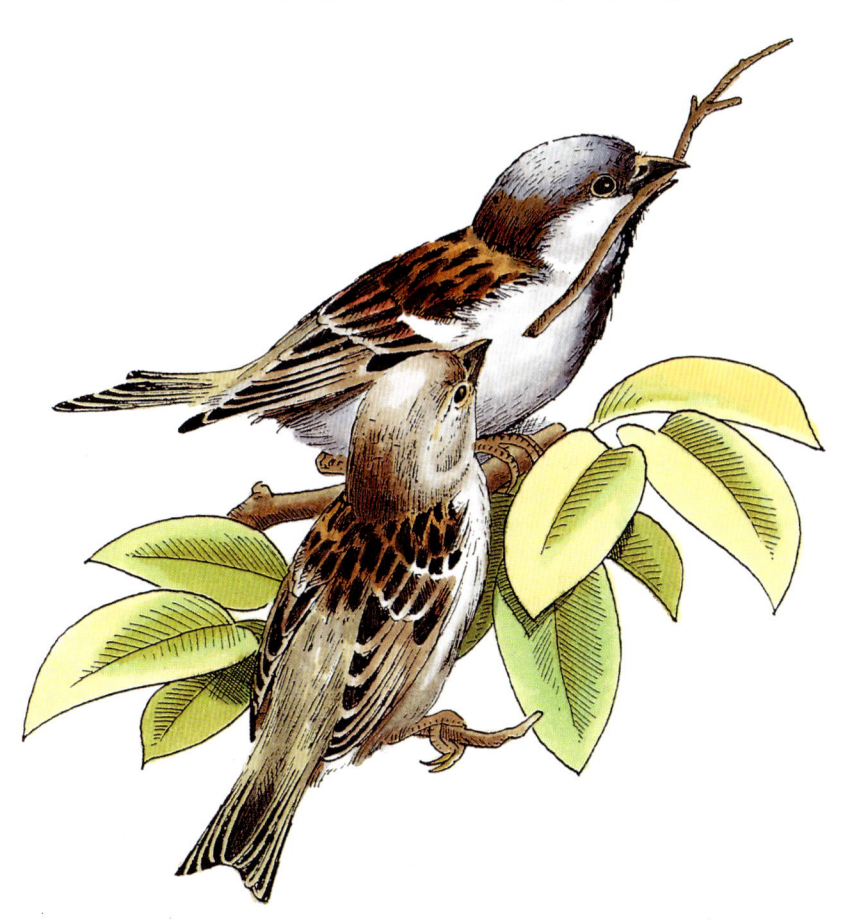

Look! Some twigs.

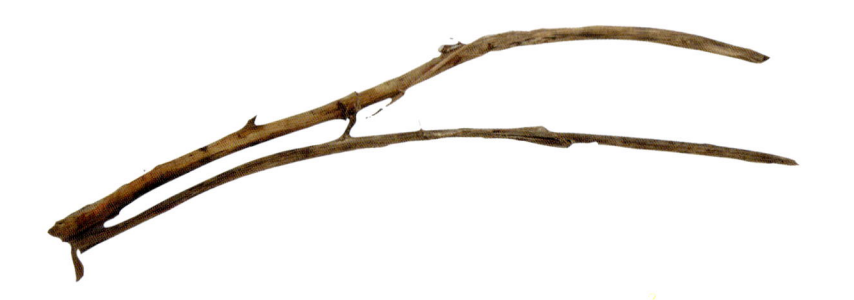

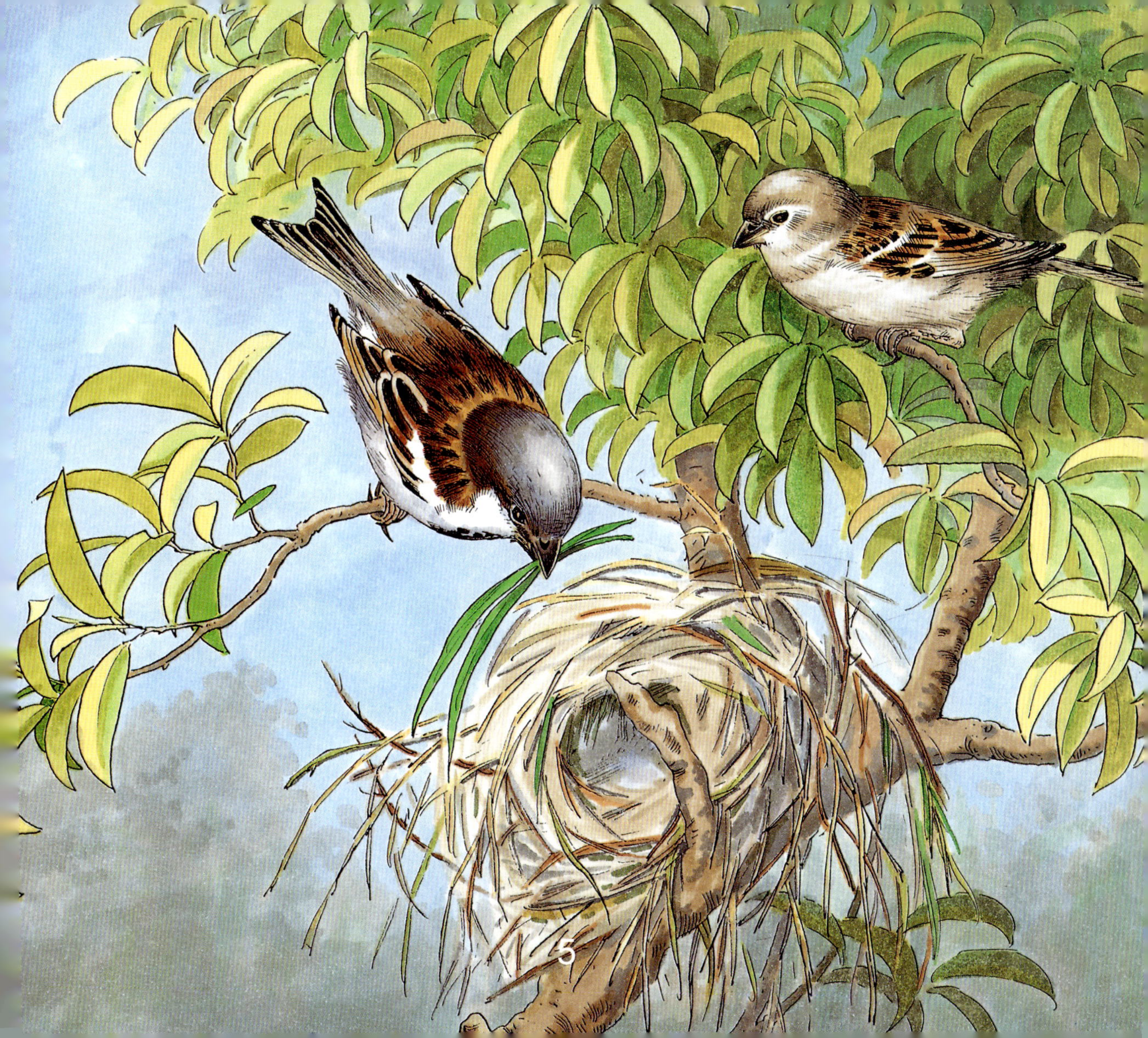

Look! Some leaves.

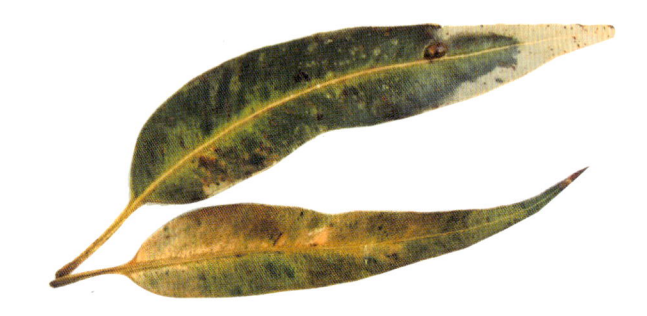

7

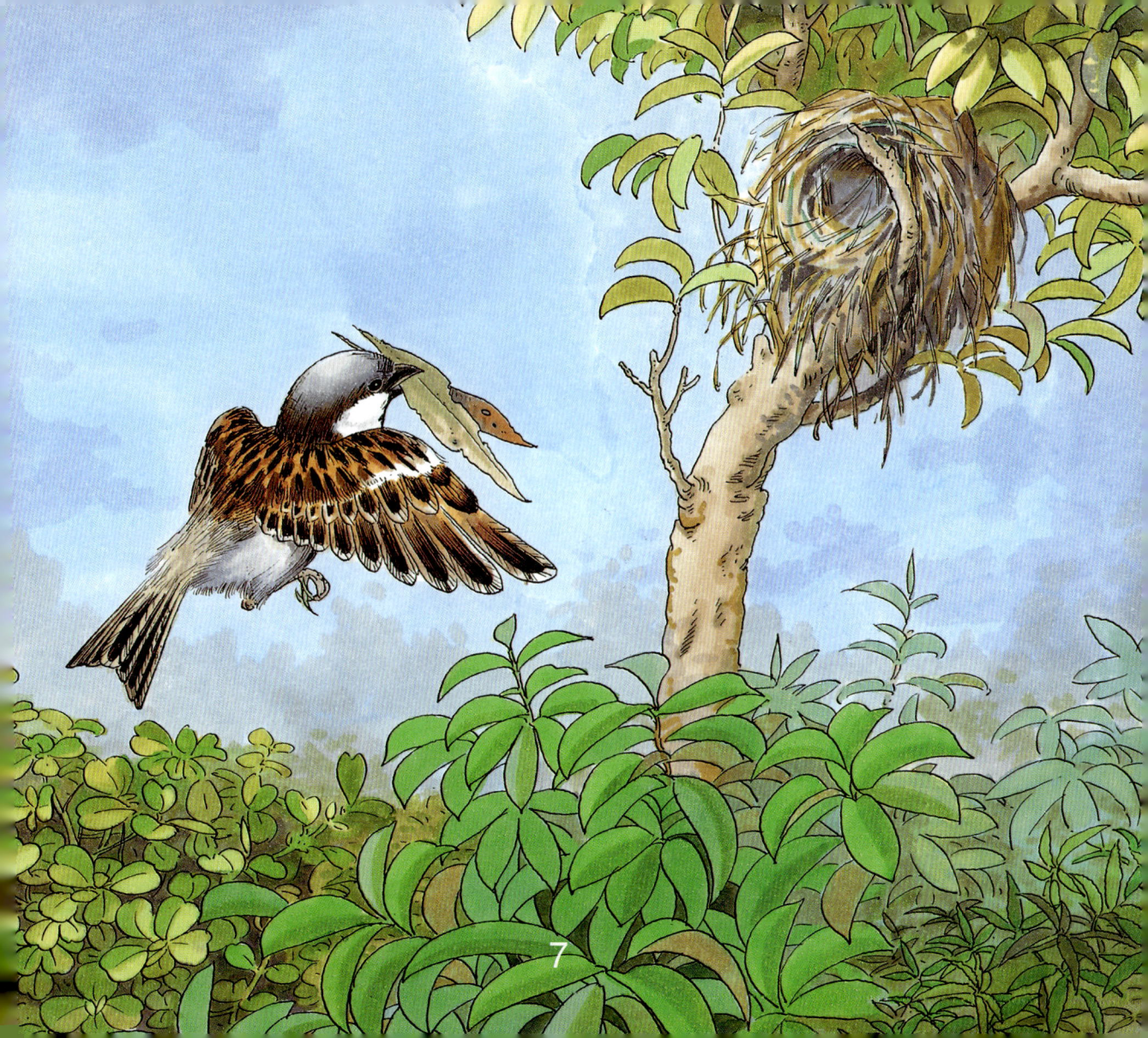

Look! Some feathers.

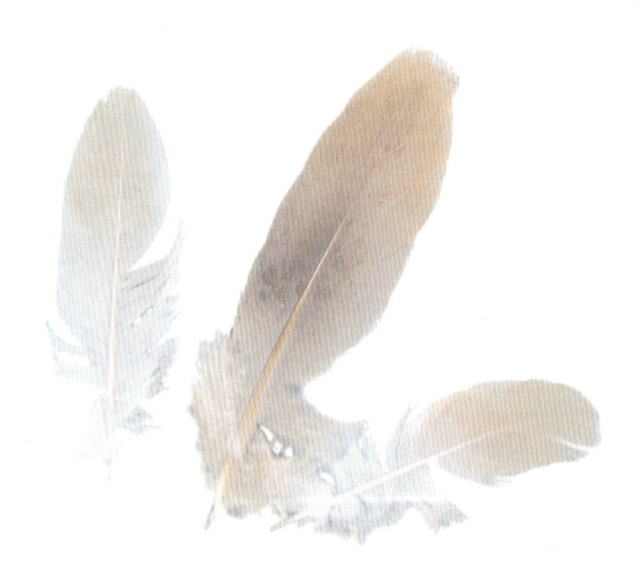

9

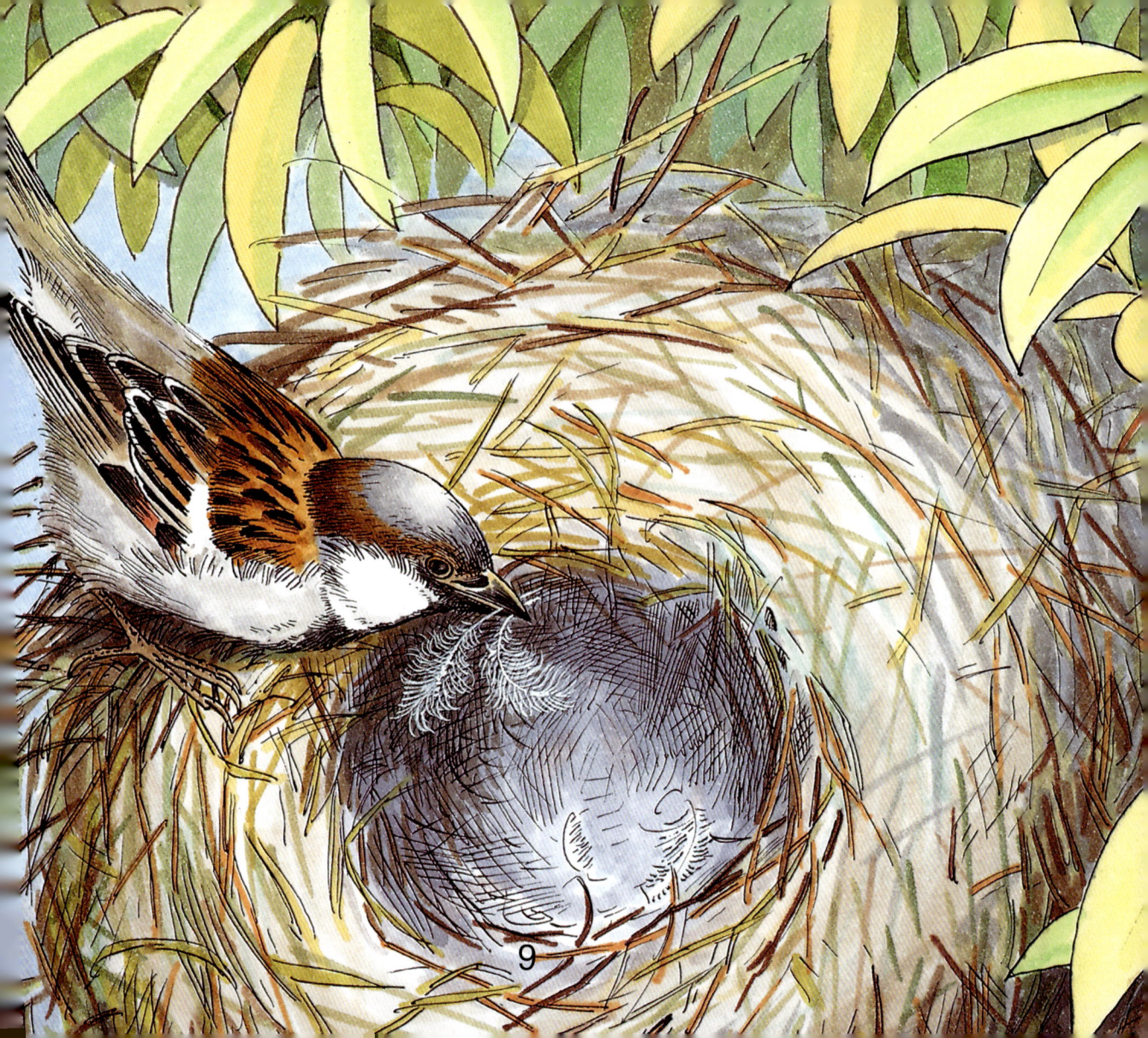

Look! A nest.

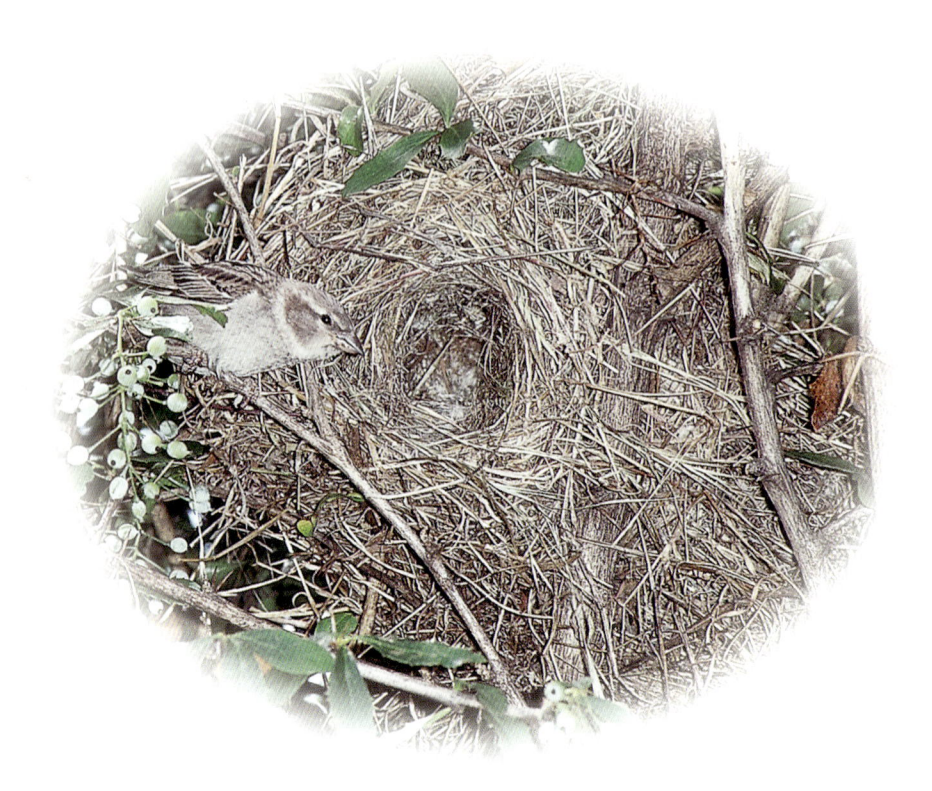

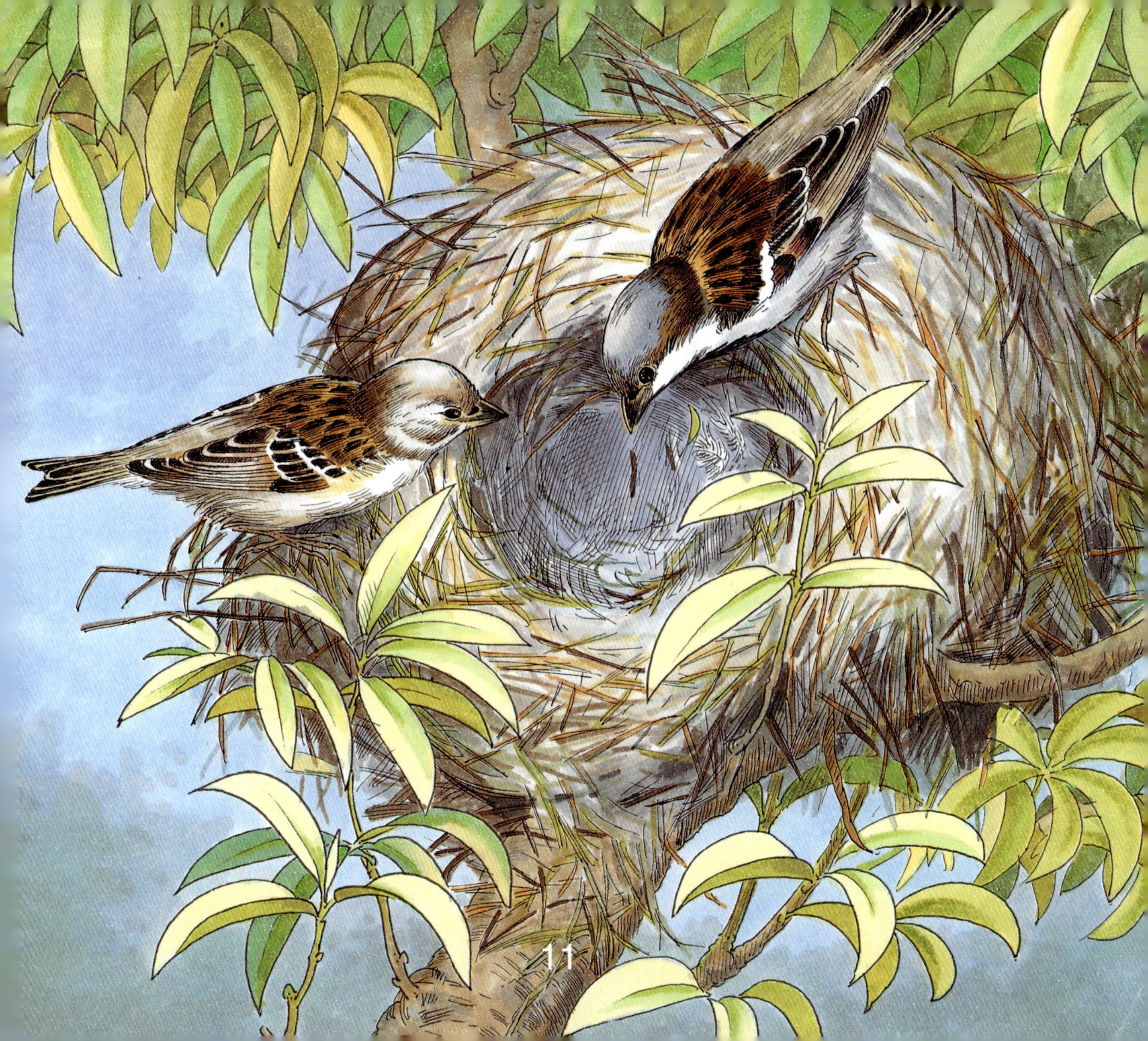

Look! Some eggs.

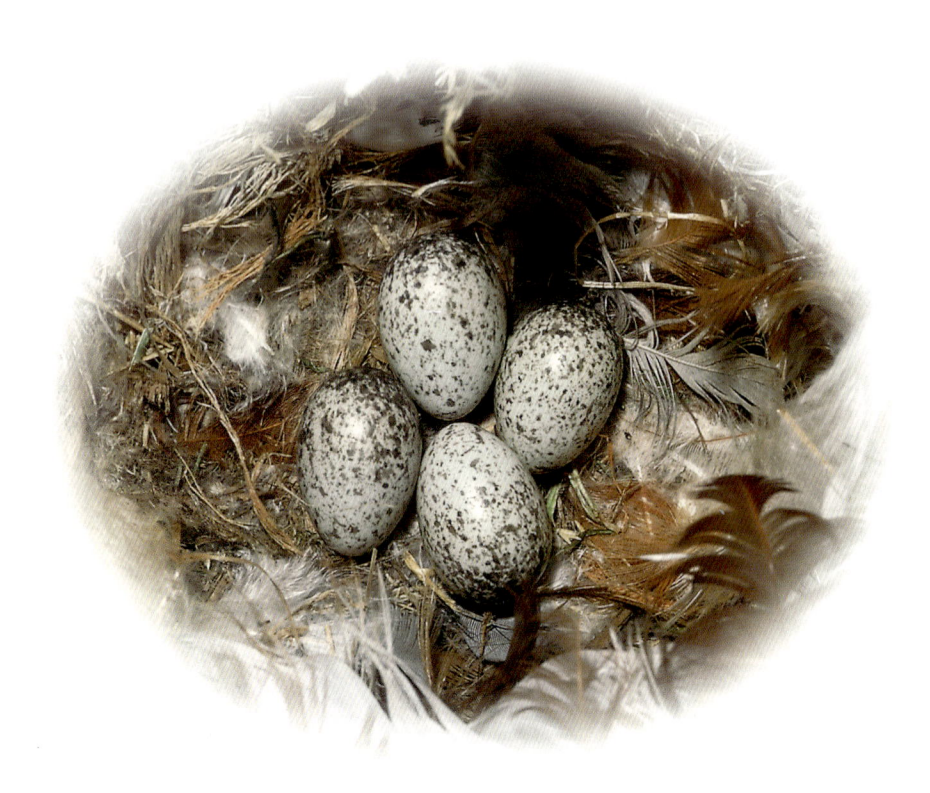

13

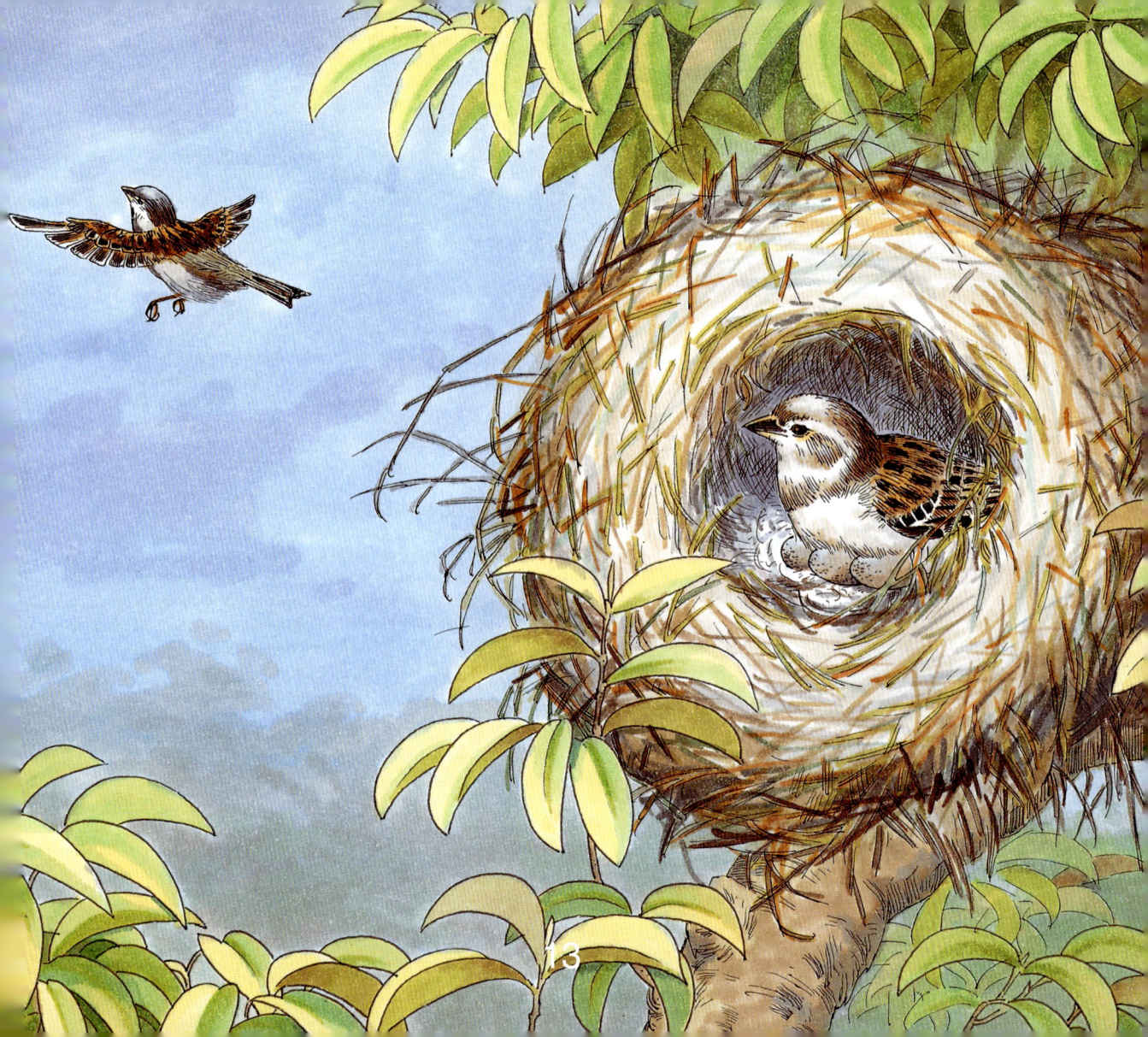

Look! Some baby birds!

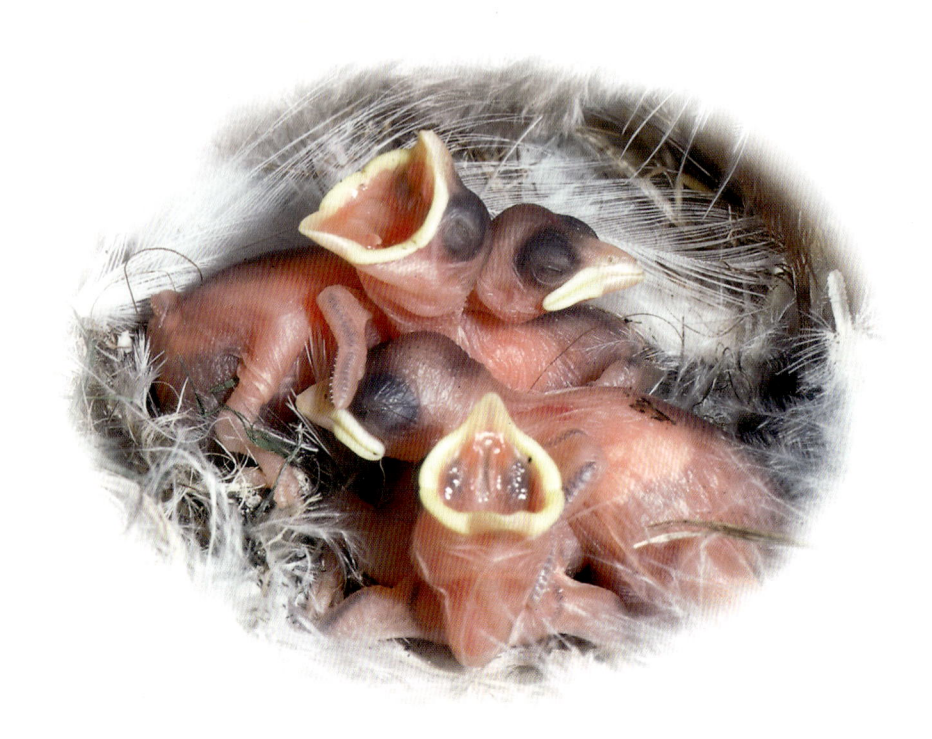

15

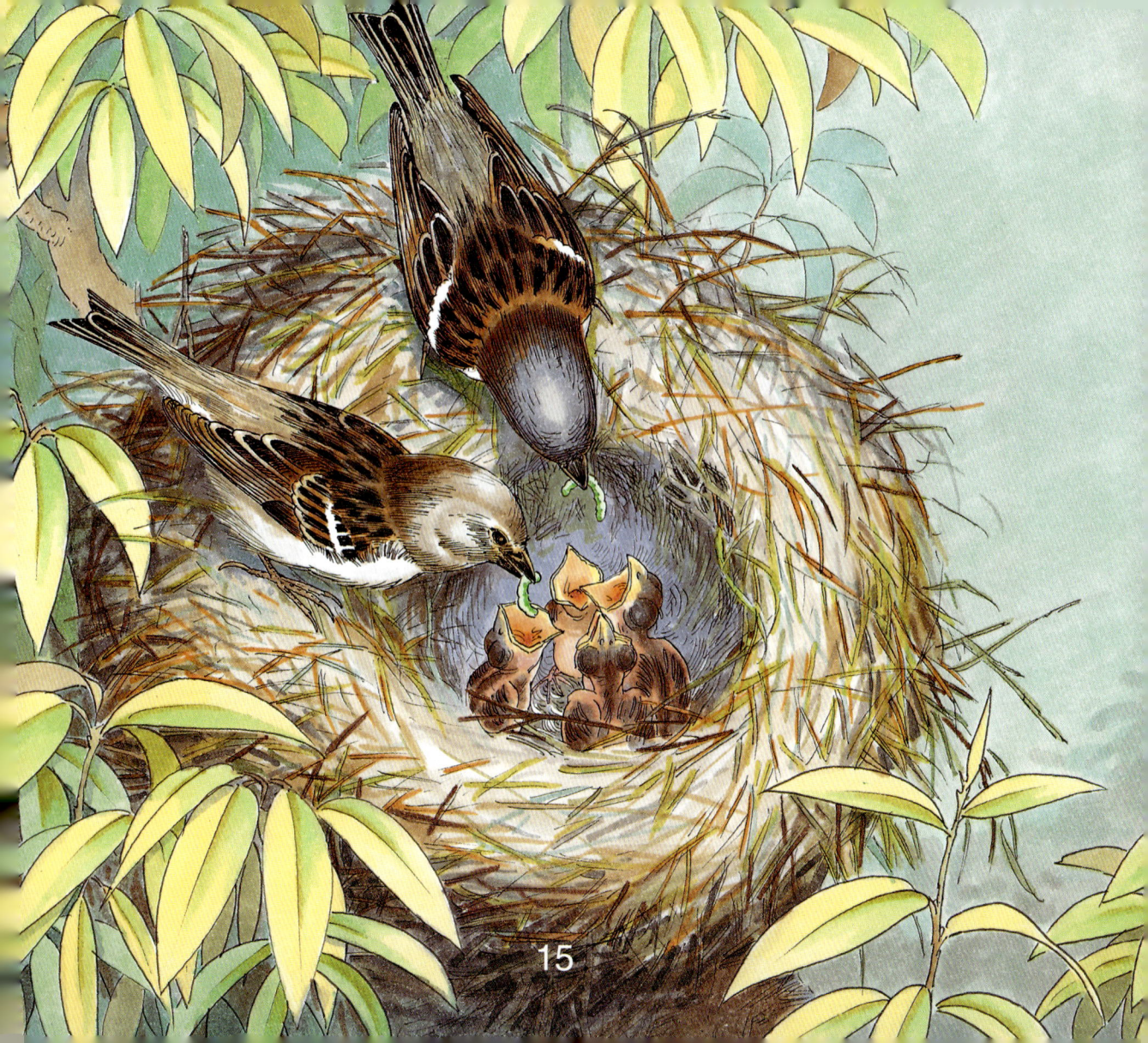

The Nest

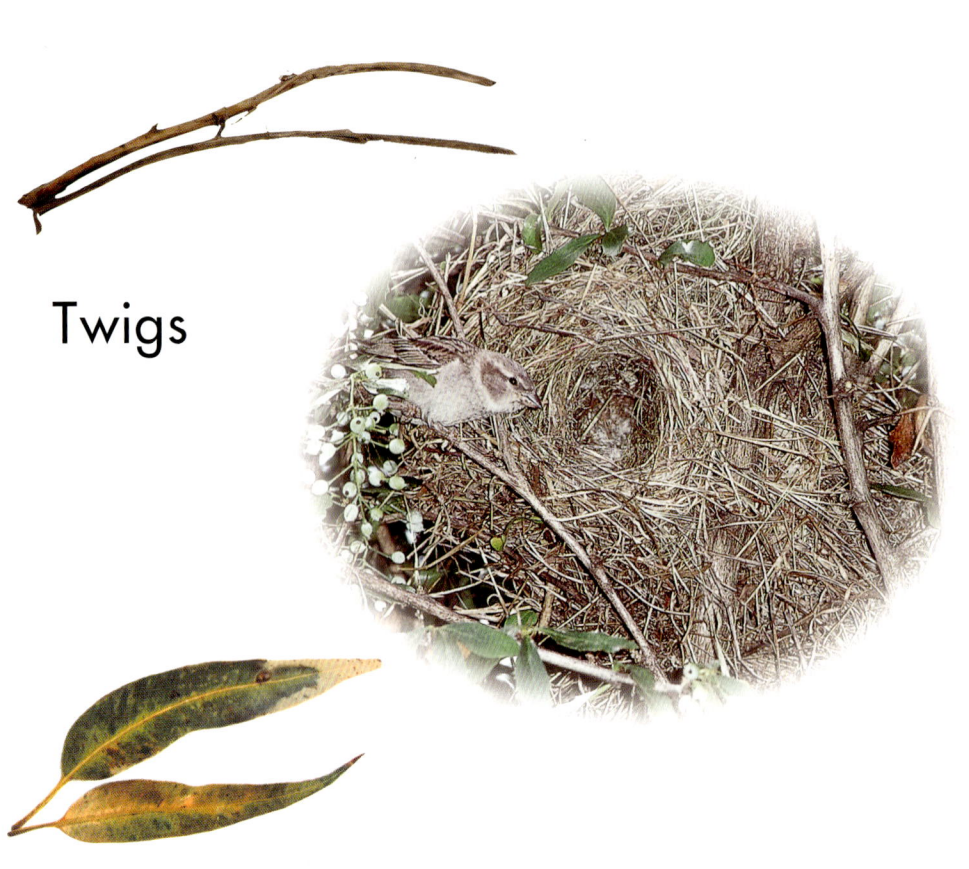

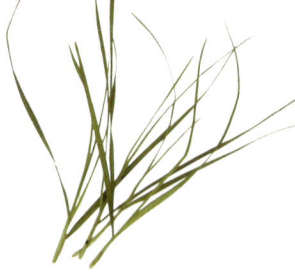

Twigs

Grass

Leaves

Feathers